Life in Colonial America

P.O. Box 196 • Hockessin, Delaware 19707

Titles in the Series

Life in Colonial America

Russell Roberts

Printing   1   2   3   4   5   6   7   8   9

Library of Congress Cataloging-in-Publication Data
Roberts, Russell, 1953–
    Life in Colonial America / by Russell Roberts.
        p. cm. — (Building America)
    Includes bibliographical references and index.
    ISBN 978-1-58415-549-2 (library bound)
    1. United States—History—Colonial period, ca. 1600–1775—Juvenile literature.
2. United States—Social life and customs—To 1775—Juvenile literature. I. Title.
E188.R63 2007
973.2—dc22
                                                                        2007000666

ABOUT THE AUTHOR: Russell Roberts has written and published nearly 40 books for adults and children on a variety of subjects, including baseball, memory power, business, New Jersey history, and travel. He has written numerous books for Mitchell Lane Publishers, including *Nathaniel Hawthorne, Thomas Jefferson, Holidays and Celebrations in Colonial America, Daniel Boone,* and *The Lost Continent of Atlantis.* He lives in Bordentown, New Jersey, with his family and a fat, fuzzy, and crafty calico cat named Rusti.

PHOTO CREDITS: Cover, pp. 1, 3—North Wind Picture Archives; pp. 6, 12—Sharon Beck; p. 9—Virtual Jamestown; pp. 10, 20, 23, 28—Sidney E. King; pp. 15, 18—Barbara Marvis; p. 17—HearthNet Gallery; p. 25—Metropolitan Museum of Art; p. 26—Hayashi and Toda; pp. 31, 34—Greenbank Mills and Philips Farm; pp. 33, 36—Library of Congress; p. 40—The Granger Collection.

PUBLISHER'S NOTE: This story is based on the author's extensive research, which he believes to be accurate. Documentation of such research is contained on page 46.
    The internet sites referenced herein were active as of the publication date. Due to the fleeting nature of some web sites, we cannot guarantee they will all be active when you are reading this book.
                                                                        PLB

Contents

*For Your Information

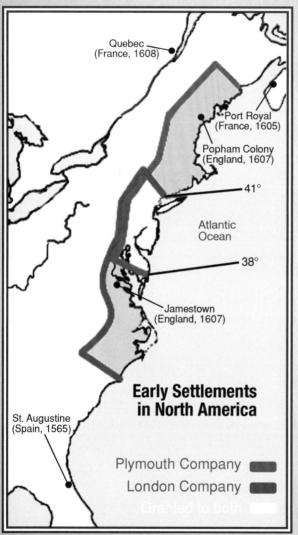

Quebec
(France, 1608)

Port Royal
(France, 1605)

Popham Colony
(England, 1607)

41°

Atlantic
Ocean

38°

Jamestown
(England, 1607)

**Early Settlements
in North America**

St. Augustine
(Spain, 1565)

Plymouth Company
London Company
Granted to both

In 1606, James I of England granted lands in North America to the Virginia Company. The company included two sister groups of investors: the Virginia Company of Plymouth and the Virginia Company of London. The groups had mostly separate territories; where the territories overlapped, neither company could found a settlement within 100 miles of the other. The first English colony in the north, Popham Colony, was founded in the summer of 1607, just a few months after Jamestown. By the fall of 1608, Popham Colony was abandoned.

Chapter

The Starving Time

    You awake on a cold January morning in Jamestown, Virginia, in 1610 with a deep grumbling in the pit of your stomach. Your head hurts, your eyes burn, and your throat is scratchy. Your whole body aches, from your shoulder blades to your feet. Your teeth chatter, because the night was cold and your hastily built shelter and its fireplace did little to keep the freezing air out. A weary chill has settled deep in your bones, and you don't think you'll ever truly be warm again.

    But you are alive.

    The hunger gnawing at the pit of your stomach makes you naturally think of food. You remember breakfasts in your home country of England . . . a bowl of hot porridge, perhaps, with steam rising out of it. Wonderful, warm steam. Then you remember what you had for breakfast here over the last week: a few cold, hard acorns one day; and on another, a tiny, greasy piece of meat from a rat that you had cooked the week before and parceled out over time like it was the rarest of things . . . because it was. It was food.

    But now the acorns that you had saved since autumn and the rat are gone. So is the small snake that you had been fortunate enough to catch and eat. It was unusual to find any animals out in the middle of winter, whose icy breath hung on to every plant and tree like death. Luckily you had seen the snake slithering along and managed to capture it. You had made it last as long as you could, eating small pieces of it at a time, savoring each tiny morsel like it was the finest steak. But now it's gone, and so is everything else. You have nothing to eat. Nothing.

But you are alive.

The same cannot be said of many of your fellow colonists who had come to the New World, sponsored by the Virginia Company of London back in England. You had come to this strange, untamed place in the spring of 1607, hoping for riches. You and others had hoped to find precious metals like gold and silver in Virginia. It was the chance to make your fortune, and so you had risked all and traveled here. You had not expected that you would have to learn how to grow and catch your own food. You were not a farmer or hunter . . . neither were many of the others who ventured here with you. You were a hatmaker, and many of the others had similar skills. You were trades-men—not farmers.

Food supplies from your ship dwindled quickly after your arrival. For a while you and your fellow colonists had lived on a cup or two of porridge a day, made with grain that had been brought from England, plus whatever you could catch from the nearby waters. But instead of learning from the local natives how to grow or hunt for food, you had panned for gold in the streams. Gold! Now you would give all the gold in the world for just a little bit of food. If only you had learned how to plant crops, catch fish, or hunt for game. But you and the others had not. Instead, you had depended on the natives to bring food. When they were on friendly terms, that had worked well. Now that relations with them had soured, that supply line had dried up.

For a while after you first landed, things had gotten better. In September 1608, John Smith had taken over leadership of the colony, which had stopped all the arguing that had gone on before. In particular, Smith and Edward-Maria Wingfield, the first president of the council that governed Jamestown, intensely disliked each other. They had repeatedly argued. The colony had struggled.

But things had been different when Smith was put in charge. He had worked hard to better the colony. He stopped all the foolish preoccupation with finding gold and put everyone to work building, digging, and preparing the land for crops. He had also improved relations with the local native chief, Powhatan. Then, in August 1609, Smith had been hurt in an explosion—had someone tried to kill him?—and had gone to England for medical treatment. His replacement, George Percy, was a poor leader. Cooperation between the natives and the colonists fell apart. Attacks increased.

Worse yet, the winter had come on, driving the wild game from the woods, the fish from the waters, and the vegetation from the earth. Even the plant roots that you had been living on had disappeared beneath ground too frozen to dig into.

Edward-Maria Wingfield was born in London in 1550. After a few years of military service, he became one of the chief financial contributors to the Virginia Company. He was the only company leader to go to Jamestown to keep an eye on their investment.

So you had eaten acorns, rats, snakes, and anything else you could find to survive. Some colonists had eaten their dogs and cats. Now there isn't another living animal left in Jamestown. You have nothing.

But you are alive.

Several hundred of the other Jamestown colonists are lying in icy graves, their dreams of striking it rich in this new land lying cold and dead with them. At least you are still alive.

But for how much longer?

You have no food . . . nothing at all to eat. Every day you've been feeling weaker and weaker. You don't know how long a person can survive without food. You have a feeling that you're about to find out.

You look at your shoes, and you get an idea. The shoes, after all, are made from leather, and leather comes from cows, so maybe if you boiled them, you could suck on them . . . maybe even eat them. You don't want to, because if you eat your shoes, then what will you use on your feet?

But if you die from lack of food, then what good will shoes do you anyway?

There is one other option . . . one other possibility for food that you haven't dared let yourself think about until now. This is something that some of your fellow colonists

Sidney E. King's version of Jamestown during the Starving Time, painted in 1957. During the Starving Time, hungry colonists would do anything to get food, including venture into areas that were unsafe. Sometimes this rashness cost them their lives.

have talked about doing: Eating the bodies of those who have died. You can't do that . . . can you? Isn't that cannibalism? Isn't that a sin?

 But you are so hungry . . . and you have nothing at all to eat.

 Should you eat your shoes? Should you eat a dead human body? If you don't, will you die? What should you do?

 Outside, the frigid January wind howls. This is the starving time in Jamestown.

  The story above depicts conditions in the Jamestown colony during the "Starving Time," which occurred during the winter of 1609–1610. The settlers were so desperate for food that they ate every living animal in the colony. Some colonists were so hungry that they ran away to seek help with the local Native American tribes. Many were killed. Another settler, wild with hunger, killed his wife and ate her body. It was truly a desperate time in Jamestown.

The Lost Colony at Roanoke

Imagine going ashore from a ship and expecting to find over 113 people, but not finding a thing: no people, no bodies, no homes . . . nothing. Worse yet, the only clue to their whereabouts is so puzzling that no one can ever figure it out . . . even 400 years later. That's the mysterious case of the Lost Colony of Roanoke Island.

The Roanoke colonists landed on Roanoke Island, on the coast of North Carolina, in July 1587. It was organized by Sir Walter Raleigh and commanded by John White. With White were 113 people, including several families. It was to be the first English settlement in the New World.

On August 18 the first English child was born in the New World when White's daughter Eleanor, wife of Ananias Dare, gave birth to a daughter. The baby was named Virginia Dare.

Shortly thereafter, on August 27, White set sail for England for more supplies. It was the last time he ever saw any of the colonists, including his granddaughter. When he returned in 1590, having been delayed from coming back by storms and war between Spain and England, all trace

Map of Roanoke by John White

of the colonists was gone. All that he found were the letters *CRO* carved in a tree, and the word *Croatoan* carved in another spot.

In the four centuries since the colony's disappearance, there have been many theories about what happened to the colonists. Were they the victims of an attack by Native Americans? Wiped out by a disease? Killed by a natural disaster like a hurricane? Starved to death? If so, where were the bodies? Or did they move their entire colony north or south, having decided that they couldn't survive on Roanoke Island? Did they move south to Croatan Island? Or possibly north to the Chesapeake Bay region?

Over 400 years later, the only thing certain is that the fate of the Lost Colony is still a mystery.

The original 13 British colonies were stretched up and down the Atlantic coast of America. Eventually, however, the colonists started moving west. Even the Proclamation Line of 1763, which prohibited the colonists from expanding west, did little to keep them from crossing the Appalachian Mountains.

Chapter

Coming to America

The population of colonial America enjoyed an enormous growth spurt in the eighteenth century as more and more people arrived from Europe. In 1700, the number of nonnative people living in America totaled about 250,000. Most of the settlements were located up and down the Atlantic coast. Within thirty years the population had swelled to 629,000, and by 1750 it numbered 1,170,000, helping to fuel the rapid growth of cities such as Philadelphia and Boston.

However, the growing population was not distributed evenly. Out of the thirteen American colonies, the two with the most people were Virginia and Maryland. Massachusetts, Connecticut, and Rhode Island also had a sizable number, as did rapidly growing Pennsylvania. Georgia had the smallest population.

At the beginning of the eighteenth century, the overwhelming majority of nonnative people living in America were English. The English settlers had been able to firmly establish their culture and way of life in America. However, over the next few decades, the ethnic character of the population changed so that by the beginning of the American Revolution (1775), half of the people who lived south of New England were non-English, such as Germans, Scotch, Scotch-Irish, and Swiss.

Ironically, it was the failure of English society at home that made English colonies succeed in America. Countries in which people were more prosperous, such as the Netherlands, did not have as many people eager to relocate to the New World. But England had many poor and wretched people with no prospects, whose very presence was resented by the upper classes. They were lured to America by "spirits," recruiting agents assigned to gather lower-class people to send to America. Spirits used candy to trick children to board a ship, and spun fabulous tales of life in the New World to mislead others. When all else failed, they physically forced weak or drunk adults on board ship. As the Spanish ambassador said of the English colonization effort in 1611: "Their principal reason for colonizing these parts is to give an outlet to so many idle, wretched people as they have in England, and thus prevent the dangers that might be feared of them."[1]

Without a pressing need, there was no reason for people to leave their home country. It was risky to come to America. The sea voyage across the Atlantic Ocean took two or three difficult months. The food was horrible, often spoiled by insects or worms. Storms battered ships. The passengers were often shut up in tiny, cramped, virtually airless compartments belowdecks, where personal hygiene was nonexistent.

It is a popular myth that most of those who initially came to colonial America were farmers. This was not actually the case. The majority of people who initially came to the New World, from the Pilgrims who settled in Massachusetts and other parts of New England to those who went to Virginia and farther south, were tradesmen, such as barrel makers, tailors, or shoemakers. Others, such as those at Jamestown, were people looking for a quick way to get rich.

No matter why they came, one thing the colonists found when they arrived in America was that they had to work—hard. England had a worker surplus (too many people for too few jobs), so people normally averaged about four hours of work per day there. In America it was very different. Continuous work all day was necessary if a person wanted to survive. There was abundant wood with which to build houses and burn in fireplaces, acres of ground in which to plant crops, and plenty of wild game to hunt for food, but a person had to do these things for himself and his family. Those who did not or could not either died or returned to their home country.

The first thing that people had to do when they arrived in America was find shelter, so early homes were quickly built. Colonists had no time to plan elaborate houses—even if they knew how to build them, which most did not.

In New York, Massachusetts, and Pennsylvania, early settlers often lived in houses made of earth. One type of home was really just a hole dug into the ground; another type was dug into the side of an embankment. These homes had a fireplace in the rear for heat and light. The earthen walls were strengthened with wood to guard against cave-ins.

Some New England settlers also initially used wigwams. In this type of house, poles were stuck into the ground, bent over at the top, and fastened together. Skins or bark were used to cover it. The rounded house resembled a loaf of bread.

One of the first orders of business upon coming to America was finding shelter from the elements. Many houses were made of overlapping bark. A house didn't have to look pretty, as long as it kept its occupants safe and dry.

In the southern colonies where temperatures were warmer, shelters did not have to be as sturdy. Southern settlers also used wigwams, but sometimes they would simply resort to stretching out a piece of sailcloth attached to four trees or poles as a roof. They'd build the walls with whatever they could find.

The doorways of early colonial American homes were deliberately small so that everyone who entered had to bend over at the waist. This way, unfriendly visitors were easier to disarm. Another defense against enemies barging in was the door latch. A string from inside the house was connected to the latch and fed through a small hole to the outside. If the latch string was hung out, then the person outside was welcome to come in. If it was not hung out, it meant keep out.

Wooden homes were often built so quickly, they wound up very drafty. As one person who spent a night in 1679 in a house in New Jersey said: "We had a fire, [but the house was] so wretchedly constructed that if you are not so close to the fire as almost to burn yourself, you cannot keep warm, for the wind blows through everywhere."[2]

The fireplace was the center of the colonial house. It was used every day. Fireplaces were quite large because they had to perform several different functions. On one side of main center fire, hot embers were raked over, and a kettle was placed above them. The other side contained another, smaller fire, which was used to heat the oven above it. When food such as meat needed to be roasted over an open fire, it was put onto a spit and turned by hand. Sometimes colonists would use a dog to turn the spit. They would place the dog in a cage with a wheel attached to the spit, much like a hamster's cage and wheel today. As the dog moved, it turned the spit. However, since it was hot work and the dog had to be little to fit into the cage—and the spit usually had a heavy piece of meat on it—it was not easy for the dog to turn it. The animal quickly grew to dislike the task. Thereafter, whenever the dog knew that it was roasting day (possibly by the smell of the meat being prepared), he or she would hide.

The colonial home was designed to be self-sufficient, depending barely upon the world outside its front door. Most colonists had little time or money to spend on luxuries; something was used until it broke, then it was repaired and reused until it finally wore out. As a matter of convenience and economy, when colonists did need to make something, they used whatever material was available. For example, in New England a craftsman

The fireplace was used for light, warmth, and cooking. A movable arm, called a crane, held a huge kettle that often was filled with stew. To ladle the food, a person could use the crane to swing the pot out of the fireplace and over the hearth.

called a wood turner used wood—usually poplar or linden—to make plates and other dining utensils. Wooden plates about 12 inches square with a hollowed-out center were called trenchers. Two people would eat from one trencher. A custom was to eat dinner on one side of a plate and dessert on the other, so the sides were known as the "dinner side" and the "pie side."

For items that a man could not readily make, there was the peddler. A peddler would travel with a horse and wagon throughout a region, carrying a large selection of different items, such as spinning wheels, clocks, guns, furniture, cloth, buttons, and hats. A peddler also carried gossip. The

A wooden plate from colonial times was called a trencher. When making objects, colonists had to use whatever material was available, and wood was all around them.

surest way for someone to find out what their neighbor was doing was to ask the peddler.

African slavery was an unfortunate part of colonial America. However, initially slavery was a small enterprise; like a festering sore, it spread over time. The people who performed much of the hard labor in early colonial America were not slaves, but indentured servants.

An indentured servant was someone who took out credit for his passage to America. He or she would have to work for the person who had actually paid for their trip. Indentured servants existed in a holding pattern: They received no pay directly, and they could not begin their own lives until their debt was paid.

One estimate is that at least half the people who went to colonies south of New England were indentured servants. The first great tobacco empires of Maryland and Virginia were built upon the backs of indentured servants. In 1755, the governor of Maryland said: "The planters' fortunes here consist in the number of their servants (who are purchased at high rates) much as the estates of an English farmer do in the multitude of cattle."[3]

John Smith

One of the most important people in early colonial history was Captain John Smith of the Jamestown colony. Without his firm and steady leadership, the colony may not have survived. Smith's fame lives on today, several centuries after his death.

Captain John Smith

He was born in England in 1580. Running off to sea at age sixteen, he then fought for several different countries, including France and Hungary.

In 1604 he returned to England and got involved in the plan to colonize Virginia. In December 1606, Smith set sail for the New World with the first group of Jamestown settlers. According to some historians, Smith was such a disruption on the voyage from England to America that Captain Christopher Newport planned to execute him once they arrived in Virginia. But once the ships arrived, it was discovered that Smith was to be one of the leaders of the colony, so Newport could not act.

In December 1607, Smith was captured and brought before the Native American chief Powhatan. However, according to Smith, just as he was about to be executed, Powhatan's daughter Pocahontas saved him. Whether or not she actually did is a subject of much historical controversy, but the story has become famous.

Smith's subsequent friendship with Powhatan helped the colonists trade for food with the natives. In September 1608 Smith became head of the floundering colony. He made the settlers work hard cutting wood, preparing the ground for planting crops, and doing other types of manual labor. Some may have resented working so hard, but Smith's no-nonsense approach helped the Jamestown colony right itself after a shaky start, and probably saved the colony from collapsing.

In late 1609, Smith returned to England to be treated for burns suffered in an accident—some say it was a murder attempt—and never came back to Virginia. In 1614 he voyaged to the Maine and Massachusetts area, which he called New England. He then returned to England. He died in 1631.

Coopers making barrels. Colonists had to make most of the things they needed, including barrels and casks, since stores were few and far between. Barrel staves (the wooden pieces for the sides) were also sent to England.

Chapter

Life on the Farm

Even though early American settlers were not farmers by trade, they found that they needed to master the art of planting and growing if they wanted to survive. Some settlers were able to plant on ground that had previously been cleared by Native Americans. However, these sites were quickly taken, forcing most colonists to contend with a land full of trees and other natural obstacles.

Clearing the land was hard, tedious work in this age when labor-saving devices were few and everything had to be done by hand. An adult male farmer could only clear one or two acres of land per year. One of the most common ways to do this was by girdling the trees. As John Smith explained: "The best way we found in Virginia to spoil the woods was first to cut a notch in the bark a hand broad round about the tree, which pull off [*sic*] and the tree will sprout no more and all the small boughs in a year or two will decay."[1] As the tree branches decayed and new leaves did not grow, sunlight came through them and allowed the farmer to plant crops beneath them.

Farming was more than just a profession; it was a way of life, with its own philosophy and rules to live by that stamped it as a most honorable calling. The beginning of the first American *Farmer's Almanac* began with words that were almost a moral creed: "Venerate [honor] the plow!

Husbandry [farming] was the first employment of man, therefore the most ancient, the most honorable, and, above all, of divine appointment."[2]

Initially, colonial farm homes contained two books: The Bible and Thomas Tusser's *Five Hundred Points of Good Husbandry*. Tusser's book was a collection of hints and tips to ensure successful farming, such as: "In winter at nine, and in summer at ten, To bed after supper, both maidens and men."[3]

Once land was ready for planting, there was one crop almost all settlers in colonial America farmed: corn. Native Americans taught the first colonists in America how to grow corn, which they called maize. They showed the settlers how to put three or four seeds in holes a few inches apart, and then, after the seeds had sprouted, how to build a tiny mound of dirt around the small stalks for support and how to fertilize the plant with herring.

Besides corn, settlers in southern colonies grew tobacco, because there was always a market for it. Tobacco raising had originated in the colonies in 1612, when John Rolfe of Virginia, a smoker, was unhappy with the bitter native American tobacco. He began trying to grow a sweeter variety found in the West Indies and South America. Tobacco growing quickly took root in Virginia; by 1617, colonists were shipping almost 20,000 pounds a year to England.

The first colonists depended on Native Americans for their survival. Among other things, Native Americans taught them how to grow corn, which became a staple crop for the colonists.

Tobacco was more difficult to grow than corn. However, it became quite profitable. Around 1622, Maryland and Virginia colonists began using tobacco as currency. It was even used to pay fines and taxes.

Unlike corn, tobacco was difficult to grow and maintain. Tobacco seeds were planted in late February. When the young plants emerged, they had to be guarded against frost. They then had to be transplanted in early April. As they grew throughout the summer, the plants had to be carefully watched for signs of worms or other pests.

Once the tobacco leaves were cut in early August, they had to be dried for six weeks. Eventually, if the grower was lucky, he sold his crop for a decent price. However, he had no control over the price, and some years he might only break even or perhaps lose money.

Tobacco exhausted the nutrients in the soil in just a few years, leaving it unfit for other crops. However, the farmer could not fertilize the fields, because then the tobacco buyers would complain that the leaves tasted like manure and would not buy them. The tobacco grower was forced to continually move the tobacco plants to new fields.

Besides the crops in the field, most colonial families had a household garden. Vegetables like peas, carrots, onions, and turnips added variety to their diet. Orchards were also planted to get fruit; apple and peach trees were the most common types.

Once the settlers began to understand how to take food from the soil, the water, and the surrounding woods, the colonists found themselves with a wealth of things to eat. The woods teemed with wild game, the soil yielded numerous crops, and the waters were filled with fish. Wild berries such as blackberries and strawberries grew in abundance, and honey could be gotten (very carefully) from beehives.

The colonists did not trust water for drinking, because of the possibility it was contaminated with disease. Using fruit from the orchards, colonists made cider to drink. (Because of its exquisite taste, peach cider became known as the American champagne. The highest compliment that something could receive was to be called "peachy." Today people still use "peachy" to indicate satisfaction.) Once cider became widely accepted as the drink of choice, a man was ranked according to how many barrels of cider he could leave in his will.

For something stronger to drink during holidays, the American settler turned to mead, a beverage made with honey and beer-soaked bread. (The word *honeymoon* comes from "honey-month," or "mead month." It was formerly the custom of newlyweds to celebrate for a month by drinking mead. This was called the honey-moon season.)

Meals were usually eaten without much fanfare. Breakfast was just that—a break from night's fast. There was little time to waste over breakfast, because a full day's work lay ahead. The woman of the house was often busy milking the cows during this time, so breakfast was simple: toast, cheese, and whatever leftovers were available. (On Southern plantations, however, breakfast was more elaborate, often consisting of cold meat, hot breads, roasted fowl, and other items.) Dinner was the primary meal of the day. It was served at noon. Supper was much like breakfast in that it was light, simple fare.

Eating utensils included just a spoon and knife. Forks, when they appeared toward the beginning of the eighteenth century, had two prongs but one purpose: to hold meat steady while the knife was used to cut it. The diner would then use the knife to spear the food and bring it to the mouth.

The farming season in colonial America normally ended on August 1 with the first harvest of the year. This was known as Lammas Day (as it was in England), and was celebrated like a thanksgiving day. The entire family went to church and brought with them the first loaf of bread produced from the harvest. That loaf was blessed, and became the centerpiece of a feast like today's Thanksgiving.

Once the planting and harvesting season were over, farmers had to turn their attention to all those things that had been neglected during the busy growing season. There were fences to build and mend, firewood to be cut, fields to be cleared, house repairs to be made—perhaps even a new building to construct. Making or repairing tools and household items was also high on the list. The farmer was continually busy until the growing season began once again.

If the farmer was lucky, his farm was located close to a town where he could obtain some new tools or household items. However, many farms were in isolated locations, forcing the farmer and his wife to make by hand everything they needed. Thus was a new, strictly American phrase born: *jack-of-all-trades.*

Of all the types of domestic animals on the farm, such as goats, chickens, and sheep, hogs were one of the most valuable. Practically every part of the hog was used by colonial Americans. The long hair from its tail came in handy in sewing, its intestines were made into sausage skins, and its bladder became a container

The upper and lower halves of a Dutch door were hinged separately. The top could be opened while the bottom stayed shut.

Passenger pigeons, which probably numbered in the billions when the first European colonists came to America, plagued the colonists' crops. Now the bird is extinct. The last passenger pigeon died in captivity in 1914.

for lard. Four large hogs would provide a family with enough meat to last many months, particularly during the winter, when wild game was not available.

Hogs also served another valuable function: They were trash collectors. They would wander about the streets of a town eating discarded food (and other items) before these things could rot and start to stink. To stop hogs from wandering into a house unexpectedly, Dutch homes in Pennsylvania and New York had doors made of an upper and lower section. The lower section could be kept closed to block the hogs while the top section remained open. Even today, these are known as Dutch doors.

Cattle were also extremely valuable animals. Shipped from England, they became a source of both food and income for settlers. Upon his death, it was common for a man to leave cattle to his children in his will.

Wolves tended to target the slow-moving cattle for an easy meal, which is why every colony put a bounty (a price for killing) on wolves. Another unwelcome animal was the passenger pigeon. These birds could strip a cornfield bare in minutes, which is why they were known as "maize thieves." Eventually they were hunted into extinction.

African-American Slavery

African-American slavery became the hideous and slimy underbelly of the marvelous new land of America.

In 1760, approximately 284,000 African-Americans lived in the Southern colonies from Maryland to Georgia. Far fewer than that—about 41,000—lived in the colonies from Delaware and Pennsylvania heading north to Massachusetts and New Hampshire. Nearly 60 percent of all slaves worked in the two main tobacco-producing colonies of Maryland and Virginia. Virginia contained 140,000 African Americans—the largest number of any colony. However, when it came to the ratio of blacks to whites, the leader was South Carolina, with 60 percent of its population as African American. In the North, the only colony to even have more than one out of ten of its population as African American was New York, with 13.7 percent.

The voyage across the Atlantic, with the sudden loss of everything the Africans held dear, was extremely frightening. The captives simply did not know what to expect. This was amply illustrated in 1737 when an African man who had been in America for a while teased some newly arrived captives aboard ship that they were to be eaten. Panicked, more than one hundred jumped into the water; 33 drowned.

Most African slaves worked either on farms, on plantations, or in urban settings. Slaves on plantations usually had Sundays off, and were sometimes kept together as a family unit. However, the work was brutally difficult, lasting from sunup to sundown in the awful heat. Household slaves were usually female. Their work was not as hard, but their male relatives might be sold far away.

No matter in what situation the unfortunate captive African found him- or herself, it was a terrible one.

A 1670 painting of African slaves working in the tobacco sheds on a colonial plantation

Men and women often had to work together in colonial times because there was so much to do around the farm. But women also had as many chores to do inside the home as outside.

Chapter

Colonial Families

In colonial America, men outnumbered women by as much as seven to one, depending upon the region. Any woman coming to the colonies seeking a husband did not have far to look. Even married with children, though, females were not strictly involved with running a home. While women in the American colonies performed many of the same duties that they did in their native land, a chronic labor shortage forced them to become their husband's partner in many farm chores, particularly during planting and harvesting times.

Whatever skills a colonial woman possessed were self-taught. It was considered a waste to spend money educating females, because a woman's basic duty was to marry and bear children. Thus about 50 percent of the women colonists who signed legal documents before the mid-seventeenth century had to make a mark such as an X instead of signing their name.

Colonial women were expected to bear children. A colonial woman was continually going through the dangers of childbirth, both because large families were desired and because a husband's right to have sex with his wife was undisputed. Thus many colonial women seemed to be on a constant cycle of conception, pregnancy, labor, nursing, and then conception again. Death from childbearing was the leading killer among women.

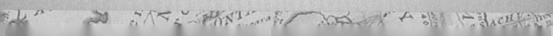

Ironically, during labor and delivery of a baby, colonial women had the upper hand over men. As soon as a woman went into labor, the midwife (a person who assisted in the baby's birth) was called, along with other women who had specific roles during delivery. One woman might comfort and reassure the woman in labor, while another might brew tea, cook, and empty chamber pots. Only after 1750 did doctors (if available) begin to be called to the bedsides of women giving birth. The men disappeared during labor and delivery, leaving the women in charge.

Bringing up a new child was strictly the colonial woman's job. However, just because she had a new baby did not mean that she could put aside her other tasks, such as cooking, sewing and mending clothes, taking care of her other children, helping her husband in the fields, baking, candle making, preparing and preserving food, tending the garden, nursing the sick, and doing dozens of other things. She was simply expected to manage somehow. As Esther Burr wrote in 1756 after the birth of her second child: "When I had but one child my hands were tied, but now I am tied hand and foot. . . . [H]ow shall I get along, when I have got ½ dzn or 10 children I can't devise."[1]

Laws in colonial times could be quite restrictive to women. For example, because they were considered too emotional, Puritan women were not allowed to discuss religious matters. They also could not wear a veil, curl their hair, or gossip. They were forbidden to wear ribbons, cuffs, or short sleeves. Under English law, once a woman married, all of her property and money came under the control of her husband. The female lost control of everything she possessed—even her clothing! One thing that a woman could do to break the monotony of her existence was to become an expert at the spinning wheel. Large wheels were used to spin wool, while the smaller ones were for flax. A woman who was very good at spinning flax could produce as much as a mile of thread in one day. Those that did were called "spinsters"—a badge of honor. However, when the word began to refer to women who did not have a man and thus sat at home spinning, the word *spinster* took on a negative meaning.

Wealthy women had more options in life than their poorer counterparts. Sometimes they managed the estate after the death of their husband, such as Martha Custis did before marrying George Washington in 1759. In 1732, Mrs. Andrew Galbraith of Donegal, Pennsylvania, took part in her husband's successful political campaign by mounting her horse

A reenactor uses a spinning wheel called a flax or treadle wheel. Spinning was a useful (and necessary) talent for the colonial woman. The yarn or thread she spun—up to a mile a day—would be used to weave cloth for clothing, bedding, and other items.

and publicizing him throughout the region. Sometimes females operated stores or businesses.

These women were the exception. For the overwhelming majority of women, who lived simply on a farm, their lives were one of routine followed by routine followed by more routine. If the woman was unfortunate enough to be involved in a bad marriage, there was little she could do. Divorce was rarely granted; the British Crown forbade colonial legislatures to pass bills granting divorces, and the Anglican Church refused to allow divorces. Sometimes an unhappy wife's only solution was to run away. Advertisements for the return of a runaway wife were often run in newspapers.

A man, on the other hand, could enjoy a break in his daily routine in several ways. He might schedule a hunting or fishing trip or go to the local gristmill. Maybe he could stop off at the local tavern or visit town, where he would talk to storekeepers or other men. Or he might take in a horse race, play billiards, or go to a cockfight.

Although the number of children in each family was large by modern standards—between 7 and 10—only a few actually lived at home with their parents. Early death, apprenticeships, and marriage took children out of the home. Colonial children, although they were given chores from the age of three, also had free, unsupervised stretches during the day. Their parents did not have either the time or energy to watch them constantly. This sometimes resulted in situations that would shock modern parents.

For instance, future U.S. President John Adams was given a gun at the age of eight. He then spent hours alone with it, learning how to shoot birds.

Another reason that colonial children were often on their own was to give them the chance to learn how to act responsibly. In a society where the early death of at least one parent was common, children needed to grow up very quickly.

Colonial children also needed to mature quickly because they faced a seemingly unending series of potentially fatal situations, such as accidents or attacks by wild animals, that they needed to recognize and learn to avoid. In this primitive medical age, even a bad cold or minor wound could take a child's life if infection resulted. All these factors combined to establish the colonial child's mortality rate at between 20 and 30 percent. (In modern North America, the mortality rate for kids is around 1 percent.)

When colonial children played, they usually used homemade toys. In apple ball, for instance, a child put a potato or apple on the end of a strong stick, and then tried to fling the object as far as he or she could. The game of hoops required nothing more than a round wooden hoop that a child tried to keep rolling along the ground by the aid of a stick he or she carried in each hand. A grass sled was simply some boards nailed together and used for gliding along the grass, just like a snow sled travels on snow.

Children would either sleep with their parents, or, later, in trundle beds that could be slid under the adults' big bed. Early mattresses were stuffed with straw, leaves, corn shucks, or cattails. Families without beds rolled themselves in animal skins or blankets and slept on the floor.

After the middle of the seventeenth century, the American colonists were generally healthier than people living in England. The English population lived much closer together, which helped spread disease. In contrast, American colonists lived farther apart. However, at a time when medical science was uncertain, diseases were free to rage unchecked through colonial populations. Malaria, while usually not fatal, weakened people and made them susceptible to other diseases. Smallpox often resulted in a long, painful illness and an equally horrible death. Typhoid and dysentery also took many lives.

Because medicine was in its infancy, the names of diseases were not as specific as they are today. A "bloody flux" probably referred to an illness of the bowels, such as dysentery or typhoid. The word *cancer* was rarely used. Rather, an "ulcerous sore" that spread was probably a symp-

Hoops was a popular game for colonial children. The object was to make the hoop go as fast as possible without letting it fall down.

tom of a cancerous condition. *Consumption* was a general term used to describe any respiratory (affecting the lungs) condition, like pneumonia or tuberculosis. One of the most common illnesses was the vague-sounding "fever."

When medicines were given, they were often mixed with sweet substances like honey or sugar to make them taste better. For less serious illnesses, colonists had a variety of treatments. To get rid of a cold, George Washington would eat a toasted onion before going to bed. Children were given the juice of an onion that had been sprinkled with sugar and simmered in the oven as a cold remedy. Lemons were also used as treatments for colds. Cloves or marjoram was used to treat toothaches. (Early dentist signs often showed a picture of a clove.)

Many household remedies for sickness came straight from the home's herb garden. To stop bleeding cuts, yarrow was used. Colic was treated with savory. Marjoram mixed with honey was placed on bruises.

One characteristic of colonial Americans was bad teeth. Because the colonies were close to the West Indies and its bustling sugarcane trade, the typical colonial diet contained a lot of sugar. Each year, the average family went through one sugar loaf—a white cone of sugar that weighed around 10 pounds. When sugar wasn't available, other sweet substitutes were. Molasses, honey, and maple syrup were all used to sweeten foods. Besides the sugary diet, tooth care was relatively unknown. Salt and water were the most common substances used to clean teeth, but these were not very effective. Toothbrushes were around but not widely used. Thus

Reenactors show how women would boil clothes in huge pots, stirring them with a stick, to get them clean. They would lay the steaming clothes over a bush or out on the grass to dry.

tooth decay was a common problem, and tooth extraction often necessary. People who pulled teeth included apothecaries (similar to modern-day pharmacists), doctors, and even barbers.

Just like today, clothes needed to be washed. Without detergents of any kind, colonial women had their own secrets for taking out stains. One was to rub butter into them and let the garment soak in scalding hot milk. Chalk was also recommended as a stain remover. To get ink stains out, sometimes the item would be soaked in urine. Laundry soap made at home was used to wash clothes. Other washing ingredients were sand, gravel, and clay.

An event of great anticipation was the colonial fair. Part business meeting and part amusement, they usually lasted several days. They were held in some colonies just in the autumn, while in others they occurred in both fall and spring.

The main purpose of the fair was to bring buyers and sellers together. A large variety of farm animals would be presented for sale, such as horses, oxen, hogs, and cows. In addition, fairs represented a rare opportunity for the entire colonial family to participate together in an activity. There were horse races, footraces (even a footrace for women), an obstacle race for boys, and a bag race for men. There were also numerous contests, such as catching a goose or a pig with a slippery tail, and grinning and whistling contests; puppet shows, fortune-telling, and rope-walking.

Notable Colonial Women

Most colonial women were forced into very limited roles by the rules of the existing society. Women back then simply did not have the freedom or ability to have careers or even receive an education. Taking care of the kitchen, the children, and the home—that was the extent of their existence. But some colonial women refused to just sit quietly by and accept their fate. These women stood out from the crowd and became successful in their own right.

Phillis Wheatley (left) was an African who went to work for the Wheatley family of Massachusetts. Taught to read and write English, Greek, and Latin, Phillis turned to writing poetry. She was the first poet of African ancestry to have her work published in the colonies. Her first poem was published in 1767, and in 1773 a book of her poems was published in England.

Another woman who made a name for herself as a poet was Anne Bradstreet. A Puritan, she wrote poems for her own satisfaction, since female poets were frowned upon by Puritan society. Her brother-in-law, the Reverend John Woodbridge, read her poems, took them back to England, and found a publisher for them . . . all without Anne's knowledge. Anne's poems were published in England in 1650 in a book that had numerous "firsts": It was the first published by a person from North America, the first published there by a woman, and the first published by a Puritan.

Margaret Brent came to Maryland in 1638 and soon showed that she had as much business sense as any man. She raised cattle, operated a mill, and loaned money. She also obtained power-of-attorney for her brothers when they were away, meaning that she had the legal right to act for them. Later she ran her own plantation, named Peace, in Virginia. In another rarity for those days, she never married.

Mary Dyer was determined to spread the word about her Quaker faith, despite a new law passed by the Puritans in Boston that Quakers would be banished under pain of death. Caught once and banished, Mary returned with other Quakers in October 1659 and was again caught. On the gallows, Mary received a last-second reprieve. Then in May 1660 she once again returned, determined to talk about and preach her Quaker heritage. This time she was caught and hanged: a victim of religious intolerance in a land where some had come seeking religious freedom.

FYI For Your Information

Pocahontas pleads with Powhatan to spare John Smith's life.
Many artists have painted this famous scene, and they often
show a teenaged Pocahontas. Smith's diaries tell us she was
actually only about twelve years old at the time.

Chapter

The Colonists and the Native Americans

When the European colonists first came to America, they discovered there was already a race of people living on the land. These were the Native Americans. If it hadn't been for the assistance of the Native Americans, European settlements may not have taken hold in the New World, and the entire course of American history might have been different. As one historian stated: " . . . the Indians taught the Europeans how to live in the New World, and were repaid by having that world taken away from them."[1]

The settlers did not come to America with the intent of pushing the Native Americans off their land or murdering them. The London Company, for example, issued instructions to all their colonists that the native peoples be treated humanely. The hope was to make Native Americans into cultural carbon copies of the European colonists, so that they and the settlers could work side by side and help each other.

However, the settlers would occasionally perform acts of horrendous savagery toward Native Americans. Anger and hatred increased between the two groups. For example, in August 1610, a group of Jamestown colonists attacked a village of the Paspahegh tribe. They killed 65 of the natives, burned their homes and cornfields, and took the children and wife of the local chief prisoner. On the way back to Jamestown, the colonists threw the children into the water and shot them as they tried to swim to safety. Back at Jamestown, the wife was stabbed to death.

The natives did not flock to adopt European ways. They did not want to abandon their culture and heritage and turn into copies of the Europeans, any more than the Europeans wanted to turn into Native Americans. The Europeans looked on the native peoples as barbarians needing to be civilized, not realizing that these peoples had their own well-defined societies. As it became clear that the natives were not accepting European ways, European viewpoints toward them hardened.

The natives were "bad people," said one colonist, "having little of humanity but shape, ignorant of civility or arts, or religion; more brutish than the beasts they hunt, more wild and unmanly than that unmanned wild country, which they range rather than inhabit."[2] Sadly, this attitude toward Native Americans would prevail in America for the next several centuries.

Other things that made the two cultures irreconcilable were the notion of private property and use of land. When the natives and colonists signed treaties for the use of land, they both understood it differently: Native peoples saw it as an agreement to share the land with the colonists, and expected to be able to return to it as they always had, when the season demanded. The colonists expected the natives to move off and never return to land once they signed it away by treaty.

The natives were also distressed by the way the colonists attacked the forest—chopping down trees, clearing fields, and planting. This chased away the game the natives needed to live. In addition, the settlers' pigs and cattle ate grass and sometimes even native peoples' crops. When the natives killed the animals, the colonists were outraged.

The colonial settlements in both Virginia and Massachusetts show similar attitudes toward the native peoples.

When the first European colonists landed in Virginia, they found the natives there living in a well-defined culture. They lived in groupings of between eight and thirty villages under the command of one ruler. The great ruler of the native peoples in the immediate Jamestown region was Powhatan.

Each village was surrounded by high wooden stockades. Inside the safety of the walls, the people lived in houses of wood covered by animal skins or bark, and shaped like a loaf of bread. Outside the village were fields planted with corn, beans, pumpkins, and tobacco. The people supplemented their diet with fish and wild game, especially turkey and venison.

Powhatan had a young daughter named Pocahontas who was enormously helpful to the colonists. According to Smith, she saved him from being executed when Powhatan's men captured him. Powhatan struck up a friendship with Smith, and that enabled the colonists to trade for much-needed food that almost certainly kept the colony alive. Powhatan also used his influence to keep other tribes from attacking the colonists.

For a while relations between the two groups were friendly. In fact, the colonists suggested that a college be established for the Native Americans. King James I of England approved the plan, and money was raised.

When Powhatan died in 1618, his half-brother Opechaneanough became ruler. He kept up a pretense of friendly relations with the colonists, while secretly planning to attack them because some settlers had burned native crops, killed native people, and disrespected their sacred places. On Good Friday, 1622, Opechaneanough suddenly attacked. Only an advance warning saved Jamestown, but several hundred Virginia colonists were killed, including the man in charge of the money to build the college.

This attack destroyed relations between the two groups. Things went from bad to worse in 1644, when another large attack by Opechaneanough killed 500 colonists. Opechaneanough was captured and killed, and the settlers decided to exterminate the native peoples. By the end of the seventeenth century, the Native American population in Virginia had dropped from 18,000 to 2,000, and the native peoples had ceased to be a factor in their own country.

In the New England colony of Plymouth as well, relations between the European settlers and the native peoples began peacefully. As in Virginia, the natives had their own society. The numerous tribes (Mohegan, Pequot, Narragansett, and Patuxet, among others) numbered only a few hundred members each, and lived in villages that several groups might share. In charge of each tribe was a chief, or sachem.

The Native Americans demonstrated to the colonists how to successfully hunt wild game and also how to catch fish. They also showed the settlers how to gather edible wild berries, such as strawberries, raspberries, and cranberries.

One Native American who was vital to the settlers was Squanto. A member of the Wampanoag tribe, he had been captured and made a slave in Spain before escaping. He returned to New England aboard an English ship, where he learned that most of his people had been killed by an epidemic. Squanto played a critical role in helping the Plymouth colonists plant the vegetables that were featured at the first thanksgiving celebration in 1621.

William Bradford of Plymouth described Squanto as "a [special] instrument sent of God for [their] good beyond their expectation. He directed them how to set their corne, wher to take fish, and to procure other commodities, and was also their chief pilott to bring them to unknowne places for their profitt, and never left them till he dyed."[3]

Squanto learned English when he was taken prisoner by Europeans earlier in his life. He taught the colonists many things that helped them survive.

Thanks to Squanto, the Plymouth colonists survived to share a peaceful meal with the Native Americans at the first thanksgiving, and it seemed as if relations between the two groups had gotten off on the right foot.

But here too, the good feelings did not last. The native peoples watched anxiously as more and more colonists came to the New England region and took more and more of their land. In 1636 a major confrontation between the two groups erupted. It was called the Pequot War, and it pitted the Pequot natives against the settlers.

In this war, as in other conflicts between Native American tribes and the colonists throughout America, the natives continued to think of themselves as small, individual tribes, whereas the American colonists banded together. Thus the natives were more easily manipulated by the settlers into attacking each other. For example, the Narragansetts helped the colonists defeat the Pequots during the Pequot War. During King Philip's War forty years later in New England, the Pequots turned around and helped the colonists defeat the Narragansett.

In Pennsylvania, things were different, at least initially. Even though the numbers of the native peoples, the Lenni Lenape, in the region were low, William Penn recognized them as the actual owners of the land. Instead of trying to intimidate them, Penn said that he only wanted to coexist in peace. When he did buy land from them, he paid a very fair price, and he only allowed colonists to settle on land that had been bought first.

His approach worked. Gaining a reputation as a haven from native violence, Pennsylvania prospered. Even ill-treated Native Americans from other regions moved there because of the colony's benevolent attitude toward them.

Throughout colonial America, wars that aimed to wipe out various Native American tribes were waged on the Pequots (1637), the Wampanoags (1675), the Tuscarora (1711), and the Creeks (1717). As more and more settlers came and the colonists began spreading inland from the Atlantic coast, the Native Americans were pushed farther back to the west. Unable to unite and come up with one strategy for dealing with the colonists, the native peoples were increasingly left with no choice but to move.

Short, bloody Native American uprisings like King Philip's War in 1675 and Pontiac's War eighty years later did little to stop the ever-growing flood of colonists.

After Pontiac's uprising, the English colonists were ordered by the king not to establish any more settlements west of the Appalachian Mountains, and the Proclamation Line of 1763 was drawn. This respite from colonization for the native peoples lasted just a few years. English authority broke down as the American Revolution neared, and colonists once more headed west, over the mountains. Periodically the native peoples resisted, but inevitably the colonists won out, and the natives either retreated or died.

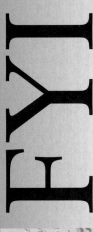

Pocahontas

There are few more famous stories in the history of colonial America than that of Pocahontas. The true story, however, is far sadder than most of the romanticized versions commonly portrayed.

Pocahontas was the daughter of Chief Powhatan, the leader of the Powhatan Confederacy. This organization governed the Native Americans who lived around the English settlement of Jamestown. Pocahontas was ten to twelve years old when the English founded Jamestown. According to an account told by Captain John Smith of the Jamestown colony, Pocahontas saved him from being executed by Powhatan's braves when she stretched her neck out next to his. Thereafter Pocahontas and Smith became friends, although there is no indication that they ever became lovers.

Pocahontas became a familiar sight in Jamestown. She played games with the children there and turned handsprings while naked in the street. In 1608 she apparently saved Smith again. She warned him not to meet with Powhatan because an ambush was planned.

In 1613 she was kidnapped by some English merchants and kept in captivity at a place called Henricus. There she studied Christianity and changed her name to Rebecca.

While in captivity she met John Rolfe, a colonist who developed the first new strains of a tobacco crop in the New World. Rolfe and she married in 1614, had a son named Thomas, and lived at Rolfe's Jamestown plantation, Varina Farms. Their marriage brought about peace between the settlers and the Native Americans for several years.

In 1616 she and Rolfe went to England. One year later she and her husband began the return trip to America, but the voyage had just begun when Pocahontas fell ill and died. She was buried in England. Rolfe returned to Virginia. He died in 1622, possibly a victim of the Native American uprising that year.

The Baptism of Pocahontas **shows Pocahontas accepting Christianity**

Chapter Notes

Chapter 2
Coming to America

1. Allan Keller, *Colonial America: A Compact History* (New York: Hawthorn Books, Inc., 1971), p. 10.

2. David Freeman Hawke, *Everyday Life in Early America* (New York, Harper & Row, Publishers, 1988), p. 49.

3. Richard Hofstadtrer, *America at 1750—A Social Portrait* (New York, Alfred A. Knopf, 1971), p. 34.

Chapter 3
Life on the Farm

1. David Freeman Hawke, *Everyday Life in Early America* (New York, Harper & Row, Publishers, 1988), p. 33.

2. Eric Sloane, *The Seasons of America Past* (New York: Promontory Press, 1988), p. 21.

3. Ibid., p. 26.

Chapter 4
Colonial Families

1. James M. Volo and Dorothy Volo, *Family Life in 17th and 18th-Century America* (Westport, Connecticut: Greenwood Press, 2006), p. 197.

Chapter 5
The Colonists and the Native Americans

1. Allan Keller, *Colonial America: A Compact History* (New York: Hawthorn Books, Inc., 1971), p. 112.

2. David Freeman Hawke, *Everyday Life in Early America* (New York, Harper & Row, Publishers, 1988), p. 116.

3. *The American Heritage History of the Thirteen Colonies* (New York: American Heritage Pub. Co., 1967), p. 90.

Chronology

1499	Italian navigator Amerigo Vespucci sights the coast of South America.
1507	The name America (after Vespucci) is used for the first time to refer to the New World.
1541	Hernando de Soto of Spain discovers the Mississippi River.
1565	The first permanent European colony in North America is founded by the Spanish at St. Augustine, Florida.
1584	Sir Walter Raleigh lands on Roanoke Island and names the area Virginia.
1587	After multiple attempts, Roanoke Colony is established. The first English child, Virginia Dare, is born there on August 18. By 1590 all the settlers will have mysteriously disappeared.
1606	The London Company sponsors an expedition to Virginia.
1607	Jamestown is founded in Virginia.
1613	A Dutch trading post is established on Manhattan Island.
1616	A smallpox epidemic decimates the Native American population in New England.
1619	Twenty Africans are brought by a Dutch ship to Jamestown for sale as indentured servants. This is the beginning of slavery in Colonial America.
1620	The *Mayflower* lands at Cape Cod, Massachusetts.
1626	Peter Minuit, a Dutch colonist, buys Manhattan Island from Native Americans for 60 guilders (about $24) and names it New Amsterdam.
1636	Roger Williams founds Rhode Island.
1652	Rhode Island passes the first antislavery law in the colonies.
1663	King Charles II establishes the colony of Carolina and grants the territory to eight loyal supporters.
1664	The Dutch colony of New Netherland becomes the English colony of New York after Governor Peter Stuyvesant surrenders to the British following a naval blockade.
1675–1676	King Philip's War erupts in New England between colonists and Native Americans. The bloody war rages up and down the Connecticut River Valley in Massachusetts and in Plymouth and Rhode Island. Six hundred English colonials and 3,000 Native Americans are killed, including women and children on both sides.
1681	Pennsylvania is founded by William Penn.
1688	Quakers in Pennsylvania issue a formal protest against slavery in America.
1692	Hysteria grips the village of Salem, Massachusetts, as witchcraft suspects are arrested and imprisoned.
1706	Benjamin Franklin is born in Boston on January 17.
1712	The Carolina colony is officially divided into North Carolina and South Carolina.
1729	Benjamin Franklin begins publishing *The Pennsylvania Gazette*, which eventually becomes the most popular colonial newspaper.
1743	The American Philosophical Society is founded in Philadelphia by Ben Franklin and his associates.
1752	The first general hospital is founded, in Philadelphia.
1754–1763	French and Algonquin Indians fight the Iroquois, allied with the English, in the French and Indian War.

44

1755	English General Edward Braddock arrives in Virginia with two regiments of English troops. In April, General Braddock and Lieutenant Colonel George Washington set out with nearly 2,000 men to battle the French in the Ohio territory. In July, a force of about 900 French and Indians defeat these English forces. Braddock is mortally wounded.
1763	The French and Indian War ends with the Treaty of Paris. Under the treaty, France gives England all French territory east of the Mississippi River, except New Orleans. The Spanish give the English east and west Florida in return for Cuba.
1765	The British Parliament passes the Stamp Act, which is designed to raise revenue from the colonies but only succeeds in raising opposition to British rule.
1770	The Boston Massacre occurs on March 5 when British troops fire into a crowd and kill five Americans. This further inflames passions against Britain.
1773	Colonists disguised as Native Americans sneak on board British ships in Boston Harbor and dump tea overboard.
1775	The battles of Lexington and Concord in Massachusetts signal the beginning of the American Revolution.

Timeline in History

1500	Black lead pencils are first used in England.
1517	Martin Luther nails his 95 Theses to the door of the Wittenberg Castle church.
1532	Incan emperor Atahualpa is captured.
1542	The Portuguese become the first Europeans to visit Japan.
1543	Copernicus writes that Earth revolves around the sun.
1550	Wallpaper is brought to Europe from China.
1564	William Shakespeare is born.
1570	The potato is introduced in Europe.
1588	Sir Francis Drake defeats the Spanish Armada.
1605	Gunpowder Plot in England is uncovered.
1631	A French newspaper carries classified ads.
1633	Galileo is placed under house arrest because he supports the theory that the sun is the center of the universe.
1643	Mercury barometer is invented.
1665	Great Plague in London kills thousands.
1685	Johann Sebastian Bach is born.
1702	England's first daily newspaper is founded.
1707	United Kingdom is formed.
1726	Jonathan Swift publishes *Gulliver's Travels*.
1740	Frederick the Great becomes ruler of Prussia.
1741	Alaska is discovered.
1756	Wolfgang Amadeus Mozart is born.
1759	Voltaire writes *Candide*.
1762	Catherine the Great becomes Empress of Russia.
1764	House numbers are invented in London.
1768–1771	Captain James Cook makes his first voyage to the Pacific.

Further Reading

For Young Adults

Broida, Marian. *Projects about Colonial Life.* New York: Benchmark Books, 2004.

Furbee, Mary Rodd. *Outrageous Women of Colonial America: New* York: Wiley, 2001.

Haskins, James, and James Ransome. *Building a New Land: African Americans in Colonial America.* New York: Amistad Press, 2005.

Perl, Lila. *Slumps, Grunts, and Snickerdoodles: What Colonial America Ate and Why.* New York: Houghton Mifflin/Clarion Books, 1975.

Pobst, Sandy. *Virginia 1607–1776.* New York: Children's Press, 2005.

Stefoff, Rebecca. *The Colonies.* New York: Benchmark Books, 2001.

Walker, Niki. *Colonial Women.* New York: Crabtree Publications, 2003.

Works Consulted

Gibson, Michael. *The American Indian.* East Sussex, England: Wayland, 1974.

Gould, Mary Earle. *The Early American House.* Rutland, Vermont: Charles E. Tuttle Co., Inc., 1965.

Hawke, David Freeman. *Everyday Life in Early America.* New York: Harper & Row, Publishers, 1988.

Hofstadter, Richard. *America at 1750—A Social Portrait.* New York: Alfred A. Knopf, 1971.

Jacobs, Wilbur R. *Dispossessing the American Indian.* New York: Charles Scribner's Sons, 1972.

Keller, Allan. *Colonial America: A Compact History.* New York: Hawthorn Books, Inc., 1971.

Sloane, Eric. *The Seasons of America Past.* New York: Promontory Press, 1988.

Taylor, Alan. *American Colonies.* New York: Viking, 2001.

Volo, James M., and Dorothy Volo. *Family Life in 17th- and 18th-Century America.* Westport, Connecticut: Greenwood Press, 2006.

Warren, Ruth. *A Pictorial History of Women in America.* New York: Crown Publishers, Inc., 1975.

Wood, Betty. *The Origins of American Slavery.* New York: Hill and Wang, 1997.

Wright, Louis B., and Michael Blow. *The American Heritage History of the Thirteen Colonies.* New York: American Heritage Pub. Co., 1967.

On the Internet

The Association for Living History, Farm, and Agricultural Museums
http://www.alhfam.org

The Winthrop Society, Texts by Captain John Smith
http://www.winthropsociety.org/doc_adverts.php

Archiving Colonial America
http://www.earlyamerica.com/

Colonial America
http://members.aol.com/TeacherNet/Colonial.html

Colonial America (1492-1763)
Stories About Colonial America
http://www.americaslibrary.gov/cgi-bin/page.cgi/jb/colonial

Colonial America
Colonial Life, Government, Colonial Wars
http://www.usgennet.org/usa/topic/colonial

Colonial Hall: Biographies of America's Founding Fathers
http://www.colonialhall.com

Schooling, Education, and Literacy in Colonial America
http://alumni.cc.gettysburg.edu/~s330558/schooling.html

Glossary

abundant
(uh-BUN-dent)
Present in great numbers.

barbaric
(bar-BAYR-ik)
Not civilized.

benevolent
(buh-NEH-voh-lent)
Wanting to do good for others.

embankment
(em-BANK-ment)
A raised mound used to hold back water or for other purposes.

enterprise
(EN-tur-pryz)
An organization created for business ventures.

humane
(hyoo-MAYN)
Using compassion for people and animals.

hygiene
(HY-jeen)
Cleanliness for health.

irreconcilable
(ih-reh-kun-SY-luh-bul)
Not being able to be brought together.

monotony
(muh-NAH-tuh-nee)
Lack of variety.

nutrient
(NOO-tree-ent)
A chemical that nourishes the body.

respite
(RES-pit)
A rest or break.

Index